Hands-On History Lab Activities

GLENCOE
McGraw-Hill

New York, New York   Columbus, Ohio   Woodland Hills, California   Peoria, Illinois

To the Teacher

American History: The Early Years to 1877 Hands-On History Lab Activities provides students with an opportunity to "learn by doing." Students work individually to make items such as candles, fabric dyes, a quill pen, or soap as their ancestors did it. They prepare foods like fruit leather, peanut butter, and ice cream. They learn to make butter and ginger-flavored soda, and stitch a sampler. They participate in oral history lab assignments and make historical scrapbooks. They make models and maps. History comes alive for students as they work through these activities. Each activity also presents some little-known facts and insights for the historical period.

Customize Your Resources

No matter how you organize your teaching resources, Glencoe has what you need.

The **Teacher's Classroom Resources** for *American History: The Early Years to 1877* provides you with a wide variety of supplemental materials to enhance the classroom experience. These resources appear as individual booklets in a carryall tote box. The booklets are designed to open flat so that pages can be easily photocopied without removing them from their booklet. However, if you choose to create separate files, the pages are perforated for easy removal. You may customize these materials using our file folders or tabbed dividers.

The individual booklets and the file management kit supplied in **Teacher's Classroom Resources** give you the flexibility to organize these resources in a combination that best suits your teaching style. Below are several alternatives:

- **Organize all resources by category**
  (all tests, all history themes activities, all cooperative learning activities, etc., filed separately)
- **Organize all resources by category and chapter**
  (all Chapter 1 activities, all Chapter 1 tests, etc.)
- **Organize resources sequentially by lesson**
  (activities, quizzes, readings, etc., for Chapter 1, Chapter 2, and so on)

Glencoe/McGraw-Hill

A Division of The **McGraw·Hill** Companies

Send all inquiries to:
Glencoe/McGraw-Hill
936 Eastwind Drive
Westerville, Ohio 43081

ISBN 0-02-822338-1

Printed in the United States of America.

3 4 5 6 7 8 9 10 11   024   03 02 01 00 99 98

Table of Contents

Landforms Affect History

The landforms of the North American continent are greatly varied. This variety sometimes acted as a magnet that drew new settlers. At other times it became a barrier that prevented their free movement. Understanding how landforms affected travel and migration patterns can help you learn why some historical events happened the way they did.

BACKGROUND

Within the borders of the United States are mountains, plains, deserts, and plateaus; mighty rivers and enormous lakes; vast swamps and great expanses of shoreline. Because the land and water in the United States is so varied, many immigrants found places to settle that were similar to their homelands. The same familiar characteristics, however, also made parts of the United States difficult to settle. You can create a salt dough relief map of the United States that will help you understand how landforms affected the history of the United States.

MATERIALS

Salt-Map Mixture
- 1 cup salt
- 1 cup all-purpose white flour
- food coloring
- ⅔ cup water (double these amounts if you need a larger batch)

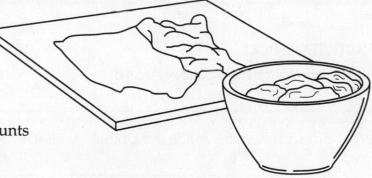

Others
- heavy cardboard or plywood
- bowl
- physical map of the United States
- thin-line marker

FASCINATING FACT ★ ★ ★ ★

More than 400 million people live in North America. Slightly more than 60 percent of these people live in the United States; almost 20 percent live in Mexico. Most of Canada's population lives within 125 miles of the United States border.

(continued)

Hands-On History Lab Activity 1 *(continued)*

WHAT TO DO

A. Draw the outline of the United States on your cardboard or plywood. Divide the map into the eight geographic regions (Hawaiian Islands, Pacific Coast, Intermountain Region, Rocky Mountains, Interior Plains, Canadian Shield, Appalachian Mountains, and Coastal Plains).

B. In a bowl mix salt and flour. Gradually add small amounts of water until the dough reaches the consistency of very thick icing. Remove the dough from the bowl and knead the dough until smooth.

C. Divide the salt dough into eight balls, add a few drops of different colored food coloring to each ball, and knead until the color is uniform. You may need to mix some of the food colors so that you have a different color for each geographic region.

D. Press the colored salt dough in the appropriate places on your map of the United States. Create the correct geographic features from the salt dough such as mountains, plains, and plateaus. Be careful not to make the map too thick, or the cardboard may warp. The map should dry in one to two days.

E. After the map has completely dried, use a marker to draw the major rivers and label important geographic landforms. Label the countries and oceans surrounding the United States.

LAB ACTIVITY REPORT

1. Name the eight geographic regions of the United States. _____

_____

2. What physical features made the United States easy to protect from outside invasions?

_____

DRAWING CONCLUSIONS

3. The geography of the United States influenced the way immigrants populated the country. With today's modern technology, how do you think the exploration of the

United States would differ? _____

4. Make a list of important geographic features in the region where you live. Then write

how each one influenced the development of your location. _____

_____

5. What major ethnic groups chose your region for settlement? _____

_____

Hands-On History Lab Activity 2

Preparing Food for Winter Storage

Native Americans and pioneers had to preserve food for the winter months. One way to preserve fruit for storage and travel was to dry the fruit to create fruit leather. Try to recreate the process of preserving fruit.

BACKGROUND

Native Americans spent summer and autumn preparing for the winter months ahead. Hunting, farming, and preparing food for storage ensured certain Native American nations of survival during the winter. The pioneers and Native Americans usually lived off provisions that were available near their homes. They salted and smoked meat, harvested corn, and dried other vegetables and fruits. If the summer season was very dry, both pioneers and Native Americans knew that starvation in the months ahead was a real possibility. They greeted spring with a great sigh of relief because their stored foods were nearly gone.

> **FASCINATING FACT** ★ ★ ★
>
> Native American cultures contributed many foods that are popular throughout the world. Native Americans were the first to cultivate tomatoes, sweet potatoes, chili peppers, pineapple, squashes, cashews, and the first to make maple sugar.

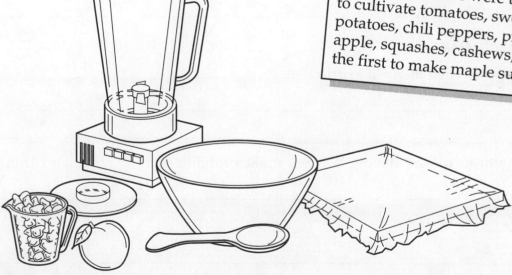

MATERIALS

- bowl
- 1 cup or more of fresh or frozen fruit, peeled and chopped
- 1 tablespoon honey or sugar (optional)
- blender or food processor
- cookie sheet lined with plastic wrap
- spoon
- oven (optional)

(continued)

Hands-On History Lab Activity 2 (continued)

WHAT TO DO

A. Wash, drain, peel, and chop the fruit. If you are using frozen fruit, allow the fruit to thaw completely. Put fruit and sweetener into the blender and puree until the mixture looks like syrup.

B. Spread the fruit onto a cookie sheet covered with plastic wrap.

C. Place the cookie sheet in the oven on the lowest setting or put the cookie sheet in a sunny, warm, dry place for 3 to 4 days.

D. When the fruit leather is dry, roll it up and store in a dry place.

E. Share what you have made with your class.

LAB ACTIVITY REPORT

1. What types of fruit could be gathered in your area to make fruit leather? _____

_____

_____

2. What other foods did pioneers and Native Americans dry for winter storage? _____

_____

_____

DRAWING CONCLUSIONS

3. What happens when the fruit is dried? _____

_____

4. Why do you think the drying process makes foods easier to store and transport?

_____

_____

5. What kinds of foods are preserved by drying today? Why do you think we still

preserve some foods by this method? _____

_____

_____

_____

Looking for the Light

Artificial light changed the way we live. Factories can operate at night. Planes, trains, ships, and automobiles can travel easily after dark. Students can do homework at night. It is difficult to imagine what life was like for pioneers without electric lights.

BACKGROUND

When the sun set, pioneers reached for candles instead of an electric lamp. Although bee's wax made superior candles, colonial Americans made candles from tallow, or animal fats, the only material available to them. They tied a row of candlewicks onto a stick and dipped the wicks into a kettle of hot tallow. A good candle maker could dip between 150 and 200 candles in a day. Because candles were precious, candle makers carefully packed new candles into special boxes and stored them where sunlight could not reach them. Most kitchens had a candle box where a few candles were ready for instant use. You can dip candles as the pioneers did.

MATERIALS

- 2 coffee cans
- wick (available at craft stores)
- electric skillet or large saucepan
- newspaper
- scissors
- paraffin wax
- pencils or sticks
- ice and water
- 1 old crayon (optional)
- long-handled spoon

FASCINATING FACT ★ ★ ★

Pioneer women treasured bayberry candles because of the sweet, spicy fragrance. Bayberries grow by the sea and are harvested only in autumn, so bayberry candles were special items. Today, bayberry candles are still popular during winter holidays.

(continued)

WHAT TO DO

(SAFETY NOTE: Do not overheat the wax; it may splatter or catch fire.)

A. Partially fill an electric skillet or saucepan with water. Place small chunks of paraffin in a coffee can to melt. Place the coffee can in the electric skillet or saucepan. Turn the heat on medium. As the wax melts, add additional pieces if necessary to bring the melted wax to a level of 4″ to 6″. If you would like colored candles, add a crayon in the color of your choice and stir with a long-handled spoon.

B. Lay newspapers around your work area to catch any drips.

C. Cut wicks 10″ long. (You may use any heavy string if you don't intend to light the candles, but use candlewick if you plan to light the candles.) Tie the wick onto a pencil or a stick. Put ice water in the second coffee can.

D. Briefly dip the wick first into the hot wax and then into the ice water. Continue to dip and cool until the candle reaches the desired thickness. Be sure to dip the candle into the hot wax and remove it very quickly; the wax will begin to melt off the wick if it is left in the hot wax too long or if you let the wax get too hot.

E. When the candle is of the desired thickness, remove the candle from the dipping stick by snipping the wick about ¼″ from the end of the candle.

LAB ACTIVITY REPORT

1. What other everyday products or services that we often take for granted were not available in early America? _____

_____

2. Explain why pioneers rose with the sun and often went to bed very early. _____

_____

_____

DRAWING CONCLUSIONS

3. What activities would you have to give up if you had only candlelight or firelight to see by? How do you think your life would change? _____

_____

4. Pioneers often put a mirror or a piece of polished metal behind their candles. What purpose do you think these things served? _____

_____

Exploring New Foods

Between the 1400s and the 1600s, world exploration added new foods, such as chocolate and ice cream, to European tables.

BACKGROUND

Americans have a true passion for ice cream. On average Americans eat more ice cream than any other nationality—about 14 quarts of ice cream per person each year! No one knows for sure exactly when or which explorer brought ice cream back to Europe, but the Italians are credited with making it popular. Ice cream probably originated in the 1600s before refrigeration. That meant that ice cream could only be made in winter when there was ice on lakes and rivers. You can make ice cream the old-fashioned way.

FASCINATING FACT ★ ★ ★

The first ice cream factory was built in Baltimore by Jacob Fussell in 1851.

MATERIALS

- clean, empty coffee can with lid
- scissors
- wire whisk
- heavy paper grocery bag
- bucket
- long-handled wooden spoon
- bowl
- 5 pound bag of ice
- hammer
- 2½ cups table salt
- towel

ICE CREAM INGREDIENTS

- 1 egg
- 1 cup heavy cream
- 1 teaspoon vanilla
- ⅔ cup sugar
- 2 cups half-and-half

(continued)

Hands-On History Lab Activity 4 (continued)

WHAT TO DO

A. Make a small hole, about the diameter of a pencil, in the plastic lid of the coffee can, about halfway between the center and the rim. Push the handle of a wooden spoon through the hole, with the bowl of the spoon on the bottom side and the handle of the spoon sticking through the top.

B. Combine the egg, sugar, and vanilla in a bowl and beat with the whisk for about 1 minute. Add the half-and-half and cream and stir until the ingredients are well mixed.

C. Put the bag of ice inside the grocery bag and pound the ice with a hammer on the floor. Pour ⅓ of the crushed ice into the bucket. Sprinkle the ice with ½ cup of salt. Put the coffee can on top of the ice, in the center of the bucket. Add ice and salt in layers until the ice is about ½" from the top of the coffee can. Save part of the salt for later use.

D. Pour the ice cream mixture into the coffee can. Place the spoon into the mixture and snap on the plastic lid. (The bowl of the spoon will be inside the can and the handle will stick through the plastic lid to act as a handle for turning the can.)

E. Use the spoon's handle to turn the can in its bed of ice. Every 2–3 minutes stop turning the can and press down on the top of the can with your hand to hold it in place. Use the spoon to stir the ice cream inside the can without removing the lid. Use a circular motion around the sides and bottom of the can. Add more ice and salt as the ice melts. When the mixture becomes hard to stir, your ice cream is ready. Cover the bucket with a towel and let it sit for 10–15 minutes. Then carefully remove the coffee can from the ice, remove the plastic lid, and use the wooden spoon to dish up ice cream made as our ancestors did it.

LAB ACTIVITY REPORT

1. How long did it take to make the ice cream? _____

2. Did your ice cream taste different from commercial ice cream? _____

3. What ingredients might today's ice cream have that weren't in the ice cream early

   Americans made? _____

   _____

DRAWING CONCLUSIONS

4. Why do you think early Americans added salt to the ice when they made ice cream? (Hint: Think about whether freshwater or salt water freezes at a lower temperature.)

   _____

Hands-On History Lab Activity 5

Come to America!

The Virginia Company of London recruited people to come to America and settle the new colony. In order for the colony to prosper, the company needed people to clear land, establish homes and farms, and to start businesses.

BACKGROUND

Settlers came to the New World seeking riches. Others wanted political or religious freedom. They came from different places, with different hopes and dreams. New settlers wrote about this new land, and others came, drawn by their descriptions. Think about the reasons people abandoned their homelands and started life in a new country. Then print a poster that encourages settlers to come to America.

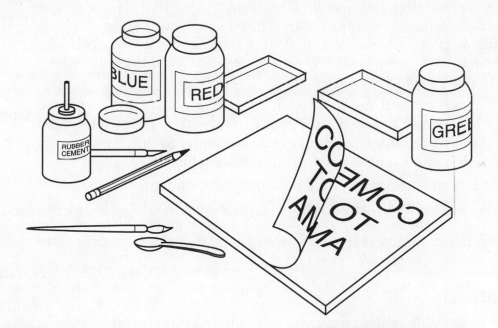

MATERIALS

- 8½" × 11" piece of poster board
- scissors or craft knife
- rubber cement
- poster paints
- typing paper
- several polystyrene meat trays
- pencil
- small paint bush
- a metal tablespoon
- textbook, reference materials

FASCINATING FACT ★ ★ ★

Virginia, the first colony, is also known as the Mother of Presidents because it is the birthplace of eight United States Presidents.

(continued)

Hands-On History Lab Activity 5 *(continued)*

WHAT TO DO

A. Identify the population most likely to come to America at this time.

B. Use your textbook and other references about the original thirteen colonies to write down things that would encourage settlers to come to America.

C. Decide on a slogan that uses one of these reasons to appeal to your audience. (Keep it short.) Draw each letter in your slogan onto the polystyrene meat trays, large enough that you can cut them out with scissors or the craft knife. These letters will become the type for printing your poster.

D. Arrange the letters of your words on a table top to spell out your slogan. Now draw lines on the poster board where you will want each line of type to go. Keep the letters straight by following these lines as you cement the letters in place. Put a dab of rubber cement on the front side of the first letter of the slogan. Now turn the letter over so that the cemented side is down and put the letter into position, starting at the RIGHT side of the poster board. Repeat the process with each letter in your slogan, making sure to leave a space between words. When you have finished, you will have a printing plate with words and letters reversed. Add decorative borders or other decorations if you wish.

E. Working quickly, use the paintbrush to apply poster paint to the polystyrene letters and decorations, being careful not to get paint on the rest of the plate. The letters must remain moist in order to print from them. If any appear dry, apply a little more paint to those letters.

F. Lay a piece of typing paper carefully onto the plate, lining up the edges of the paper and plate. Use the tablespoon's bowl to rub over the letters, making sure that each one makes good contact with the paper. Then lift one corner of the paper and peel it gently from the plate, being careful not to smear the printing. Display your slogans.

LAB ACTIVITY REPORT

1. What group of possible settlers were you trying to reach with your poster?_____

_____

2. What could have discouraged people from coming to America?_____

_____

DRAWING CONCLUSIONS

3. If it became possible to join a group that would establish the first colony on the moon during your lifetime, what would you have to consider before moving to the

new colony?_____

Copyright © by The McGraw-Hill Companies.

Hands-On History Lab Activity 6

Indentured Servants Come to America

Many settlers could not afford the passage to America. Some people, both adults and children, signed contracts of indenture in return for their passage. Contracts of indenture were legal documents that required the indentured servant or apprentice to work for the person who paid the fare for a specific period of time.

BACKGROUND

Contracts of indenture allowed settlers to work for a specific number of years in return for having their passage to America paid. Children often indentured themselves to an artisan and became apprentices. The indenturing contract stated what was expected of both the master and the servant during the bondage period. Many felt the hard work and lack of freedom were worth the possibility of a new life in America. You and a partner can make a documentary about the life of an indentured child.

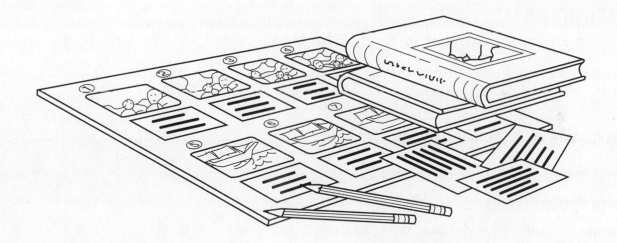

MATERIALS

- cassette recorder or camcorder (optional)
- index cards
- audiotape or videotape (optional)
- reference materials on indenturing or apprenticeship
- poster board and drawings to make a storyboard

> ### FASCINATING FACT ★ ★ ★
> In 1665 almost half of the members of Virginia's House of Burgesses was made up of former indentured servants.

(continued)

Hands-On History Lab Activity 6 (continued)

WHAT TO DO

A. Research to find out about the life of indentured servants or apprentices.

B. Imagine that you are an indentured servant or an apprentice. Write down what a common day in your life might be like. Consider what chores you would do, where you would take shelter, what your role in the family would be, what time you would get up each day, and what clothes you would wear.

C. Organize the information on index cards. Decide what information would be most important to describe the life of an indentured child or apprentice and make a storyboard, or a visual plan, for your documentary.

D. Watch a program on public television or use library resources to find a program where someone interviews an interesting figure about his or her life. Pay attention to the kind of questions that are asked.

E. With your partner, create a role play where one of you acts as an indentured child or an apprentice and the other as a journalist. Record your interview on audiotape or videotape. Share with your class.

LAB ACTIVITY REPORT

1. How many years did your research indicate indentured servants usually worked before they received their freedom? _____

_____

2. What did you learn that surprised you? _____

_____

DRAWING CONCLUSIONS

3. Would you ever consider becoming an indentured worker? Why do you think so many young people decided to become indentured workers? _____

_____

_____

4. Apprentices often learned their trades by working for a craft worker in exchange for training. Do you think such a system would work today? Why or why not? _____

_____

_____

Hands-On History Lab Activity 7

Butter Churning

Because many early settlers could not afford to keep a cow, butter was a luxury item during colonial times. Make your own butter to understand how the pioneers did it.

BACKGROUND

Making butter was usually the job of children. After milking the cow, they poured the milk into wooden tubs and waited for it to sour. Then they skimmed off the cream and poured it into a butter churn. A butter churn looked like a tall wooden bucket that was narrower at the top than at the bottom. A long wooden stick called a *dasher* fit into the churn and buttermakers pushed it up and down to agitate the cream. The cream bubbled and then turned into curds. When the curds finally gathered, or formed into clumps, buttermakers scraped the butter off the dasher, mixed it with cold water, and added salt. Then they put it into round wooden molds that pressed a design, such as a star or a shock of wheat, into the butter. Some buttermakers had their personal trademarks, such as their initials.

MATERIALS

- mixing bowl
- clean quart glass jar with screw top lid
- 5 ice cubes
- butter dish
- 2 cups whipping cream
- ¼ teaspoon salt
- slotted spoon or sieve
- crackers to try your butter

FASCINATING FACT ★ ★ ★

When the children churned butter, they often chanted rhymes. A favorite rhyme went:
Come, butter, come.
Come, butter, come.
Peter standing at the gate
Waiting for butter cake.
Come, butter, come.

(continued)

Hands-On History Lab Activity 7 *(continued)*

WHAT TO DO

A. Place the cream in the glass jar, screw the lid on, and set it in a warm place for about two hours.

B. Make sure that the lid is tightened and then vigorously shake the jar up and down for 10 to 20 minutes. You will probably have to take turns with a partner. Making butter is hard work!

C. When the butter sticks together and forms solid clumps, pour off the buttermilk through a slotted spoon or sieve and place the butter into a mixing bowl. If the butter clumps are not sticking together, add a couple of teaspoons of hot water before pouring off the buttermilk.

D. Wash your hands very well. Place the ice cubes in the mixing bowl with the butter. Allow the ice cubes to melt a little. With your fingers work the water into the butter until the butter is cold. Pour off the ice and water. Sprinkle the salt over the butter and knead in with your hands. Spread the butter on crackers and share with your classmates.

LAB ACTIVITY REPORT

1. How long did it take you to make your butter? _____

_____

2. Make up a rhyme that you could say while churning butter. _____

_____

DRAWING CONCLUSIONS

3. What other chores can you think of that were probably done by children during

pioneer times? _____

_____

_____

4. Almost no one makes butter at home today. What are some other foods that once were

made at home that are now prepared in factories? _____

_____

5. During colonial times, restaurants were rare. Now they are common. Why do you

think people eat away from home more often now? _____

_____

Hands-On History Lab Activity 8

Native American Records

For centuries Native Americans recorded their history by word of mouth and by drawings. Native Americans may have seen the American Revolution quite differently from the colonists. Imagine that you are a Native American storyteller who witnessed the Revolutionary War.

BACKGROUND

The news in early America was usually passed by word of mouth since many of the colonists could not read. The Native American culture, too, passed on traditions, values, and news orally, through the time-honored tradition of storytelling. Drawings on animal skins often retold the story. These drawings helped storytellers remember important events. Native Americans created the paints and pigments for these drawings from plants, berries, and minerals available in nature. You can record a historical event the way Native American historians did.

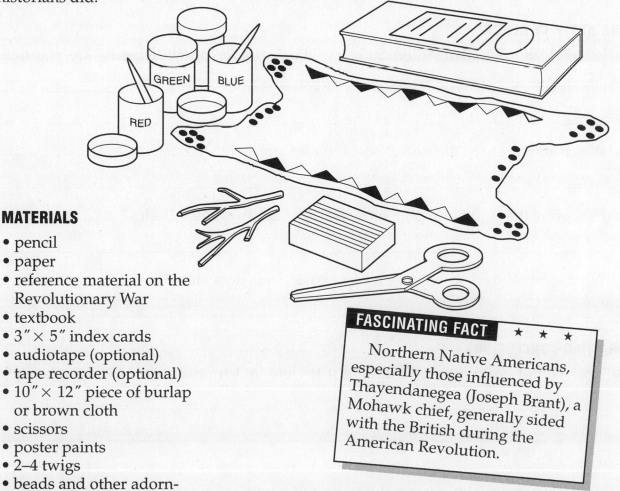

MATERIALS

- pencil
- paper
- reference material on the Revolutionary War
- textbook
- 3" × 5" index cards
- audiotape (optional)
- tape recorder (optional)
- 10" × 12" piece of burlap or brown cloth
- scissors
- poster paints
- 2–4 twigs
- beads and other adornments (optional)

FASCINATING FACT ★ ★ ★

Northern Native Americans, especially those influenced by Thayendanegea (Joseph Brant), a Mohawk chief, generally sided with the British during the American Revolution.

(continued)

Hands-On History Lab Activity 8 *(continued)*

WHAT TO DO

A. Use your textbook and research materials to learn more about the Revolutionary War and Native American stories. Try to look at the information as if you were a Native American during the late 1700s.

B. Organize your information on 3″ × 5″ index cards.

C. Create a story about the Revolutionary War that will be told orally. Remember that you are a Native American telling the story as you witnessed it. If possible, when you have finished writing your story, record it on an audiocassette.

D. Cut the piece of cloth into the shape of the skin of a small animal, such as a squirrel or rabbit. With the poster paint and twigs (to be used as paint-brushes), paint symbols and drawings to tell your story on the "animal skin" story cloth. If you would like, decorate your "animal skin" history book with beads and other Native American decorations.

E. Share your story and drawings with your class.

LAB ACTIVITY REPORT

1. Which form of Native American storytelling—oral or drawn records—do you think expressed your ideas most effectively? Explain your answer. _____

_____

2. Which animal shape did you choose for your story cloth? _____

_____

3. How were the paints and pigments created to draw on animal skins? _____

_____

4. What symbols did you use when you created your story cloth? _____

_____

DRAWING CONCLUSIONS

5. How would your story be different if it were told from a colonist's point of view?

_____

_____

Hands-On History Lab Activity 9

Pioneer Soap

Pioneers living on farms usually made soap once a year from animal fats collected at butchering time. This soap was used for everything, washing dishes, clothes, and people, too! Try making a bar of soap to understand this aspect of pioneer life.

BACKGROUND

The average American pioneer did not have very much need for a large supply of soap. Most pioneers washed their clothing only once a month and bathed even less frequently. They thought that baths were bad for their health! A harsh mixture of wood ashes, water, and animal fat, homemade soap was often a strong, soft, jellylike blob. Soap makers made soap in a large pot over an outdoor fire to keep the fumes away from the house. The fat was heated and stirred for hours until it turned into a smooth, thick liquid. The top layer of fat was skimmed off and poured into wooden tubs. Then lye, made from wood ashes and water, was stirred into the melted fat. It took several hours of stirring to combine the fat and lye to make soap. The soap was then poured into small wooden boxes, allowed to cool, and stored.

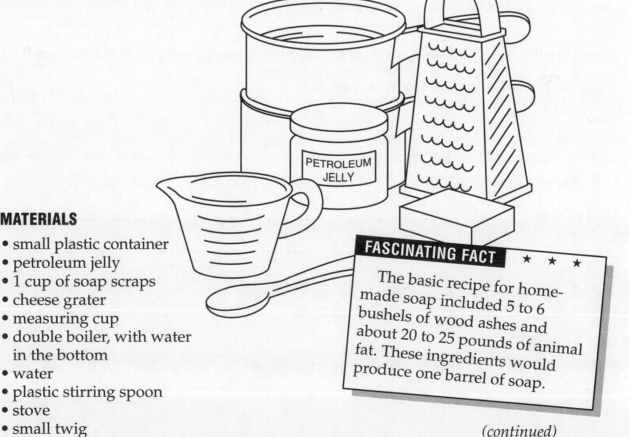

MATERIALS
- small plastic container
- petroleum jelly
- 1 cup of soap scraps
- cheese grater
- measuring cup
- double boiler, with water in the bottom
- water
- plastic stirring spoon
- stove
- small twig

FASCINATING FACT ★ ★ ★

The basic recipe for home-made soap included 5 to 6 bushels of wood ashes and about 20 to 25 pounds of animal fat. These ingredients would produce one barrel of soap.

(continued)

Hands-On History Lab Activity 9 (continued)

WHAT TO DO

A. Grease the inside of the plastic container with petroleum jelly. Set aside.

B. Grate 1 cup of scraps of soap with the cheese grater until they are about the size of pencil erasers. Put the grated soap into the top of the double boiler. Add ½ cup of water. Turn the stove on medium heat. Carefully stir the soap and water until the mixture turns into a smooth liquid. Stir the mixture every once in a while. Be patient. It can take up to a half an hour for the soap to melt. *(SAFETY NOTE: Handle hot materials carefully to avoid burns.)*

C. When the soap is the consistency of honey, stand a small twig in the mixture. If the twig stands up without support, the soap is ready to pour into the plastic container.

D. Allow the soap to cool overnight. After the soap hardens, turn the mold over and slip out the bar of soap.

LAB ACTIVITY REPORT

1. What were the main ingredients of pioneer soap? _____

_____

_____

2. How was the soap you made different from pioneer soap? Do you think the smell of

soap making was the same? Why or why not? _____

_____

_____

3. Did you use your soap? How would you compare the soap you made with your usual

kind of soap? _____

_____

_____

_____

DRAWING CONCLUSIONS

4. What effect do you think modern soap-making methods have had on the way that

we live? _____

_____

Hands-On History Lab Activity 10

The First Political Parties

During the election of 1796 the American voters had something that had never been seen before in America—political parties. Create a collection of campaign buttons and ribbons to support the policies and candidates of one of these political parties.

BACKGROUND

Political parties existed for the first time during the election of 1796, and the lines between them were clearly drawn. The Federalist party believed in strong central government. Representing the interests of wealthy, successful Americans, the Federalists wanted continued trade with Britain and thought power should be held by a small group of wealthy Americans. The Democratic-Republican party represented the interests of shopkeepers and small farmers, who wanted widely shared power and strong state government. The Democratic-Republicans supported the new French Republic in foreign trade. Imagine that you belong to one of these groups.

FASCINATING FACT ★ ★ ★

Thomas Jefferson had a pet mockingbird. President Jefferson taught the bird to sit on his shoulder while he worked. The bird followed the President up to bed by hopping up the stairs one step at a time.

MATERIALS

- research materials on the Federalist and Democratic–Republican parties
- 3″ × 5″ index cards
- markers or poster paints
- 12″ × 18″ piece of poster board
- several small safety pins
- several pieces of 2″ ribbon, each about 5″ long
- all purpose white glue or fabric glue
- compass for making circles

(continued)

Hands-On History Lab Activity 10 (continued)

WHAT TO DO

A. Use research materials and your textbook to learn about the political party you chose. Using the note cards, write down key issues that you think could be turned into political slogans for the political party or candidate. For each issue write a short slogan that will fit on a button or ribbon.

B. Cut a circle from the poster board, about 4″ in diameter, for each campaign button. Use the 5″ strips of ribbon for other campaign slogans.

C. Use markers or poster paints to print your slogans onto the buttons and ribbons. Let them dry.

D. Use the white glue to attach the safety pins to the backs of the buttons and ribbons. Squeeze a small amount of glue, about the size of a pea, onto the center of the button or the top edge of the ribbon. Let it dry slightly until the top surface of the glue becomes tacky. Then open the safety pins and press the side with the head attached into the tacky glue, holding it a few minutes, if necessary, to keep the pin straight.

E. Display your buttons and ribbons with those of your classmates.

LAB ACTIVITY REPORT

1. How did preparing the campaign buttons and ribbons on the important issues in the

election of 1796 help you understand political parties? _____

_____

_____

2. Which campaign issue was the easiest to write a slogan for? Which was most difficult?

_____

_____

DRAWING CONCLUSIONS

3. Do you think your campaign materials would be an effective way to inform voters

about the views of political parties today? Why or why not? _____

_____

_____

4. If you were making campaign material for modern elections, what kinds of materials

would you create?_____

_____

Hands-On History Lab Activity 11

Alphabet Sampler

Many American children learned the letters of the alphabet by stitching them on pieces of linen. Create an alphabet sampler the way the pioneer children did.

BACKGROUND

Many children in early America learned their alphabet on linen samplers. Often the sampler featured the alphabet in upper and lower case letters and the numbers from one through ten. Children as young as five years old worked to make perfect stitches and lessons. Stitching was an important lesson for all children. Girls learned stitching to make clothing and other household items and boys learned it for leather work and shoemaking. Often a cross-stitch, one of the easiest stitches, was used. The cross-stitch is a simple X. Fancier samplers included verses, pictures of buildings, animals, and Bible verses and a variety of different stitches.

MATERIALS

- graph paper
- cloth (heavy cotton)
- scissors
- pencil
- embroidery thread, in the colors of your choice
- embroidery needle
- masking tape

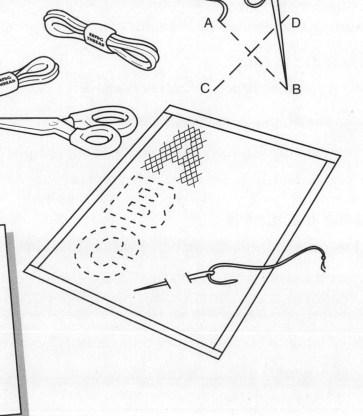

FASCINATING FACT ★ ★ ★

Samplers often contain the names and ages of the people who made them as well as the date the samplers were completed. The oldest existing sampler was made by Jane Bostocke in England during the sixteenth century.

(continued)

WHAT TO DO

A. On the graph paper, mark Xs in the boxes necessary to create an A, B, and C as shown in the diagram. Add any other designs if you wish. Bind the cloth with masking tape by folding the tape in half lengthwise over the edges of the cloth.

B. Darken the back of your design on the graph paper with a soft lead pencil. Lay it over your cloth and trace over the Xs in your design to transfer it to the cloth. Cut a piece of embroidery thread about 14" long. Embroidery thread contains six threads. Separate the embroidery thread into 2 strands of 3 threads each. Thread the needle with one of these strands and make a knot at the end of the thread.

C. Begin stitching your sampler by choosing an X on the top or bottom of your design. Poke the needle through the back of the cloth at the upper left-hand point of the X (A). Pull the needle through the cloth until the knot stops the thread. Then poke the needle through the top side of the cloth at the lower righthand point of the X (B) and pull it through the back side of the cloth (see diagram). The result should look like \. Repeat the procedure, making the stitch go in the opposite direction, like /(C to D). The stitch should look like an X when you are done. Continue stitching the pattern you have traced on the cloth until you have created an A, B, and C.

LAB ACTIVITY REPORT

1. What was the purpose of pioneer samplers? _____

_____

2. How long did it take you to complete your sampler? _____

_____

DRAWING CONCLUSIONS

3. How does the way the alphabet was learned during the 1800s differ from the way it is

learned today? Why do you think it is different? _____

_____

4. What kinds of home activities help students learn reading and writing skills in

today's world? _____

_____

_____

Homespun Dyes

Pioneers took great pride in the dyes they created. Try to create dye using natural products around you.

BACKGROUND

After pioneer women carded, or straightened, wool fibers, the yarn was ready for dyeing. Blue dye, made from indigo, was a favorite among pioneer women. They spent hours under the shade trees tending huge pots of dye to get just the right hue. Until the middle of the nineteenth century, all dyes were derived from natural sources such as twigs, leaves, and berries. The first book on dyeing published in the United States was called the *Country Dyer's Assistant*. Published in 1798, it listed ingredients such as olives, walnut shells, barks, and gooseberries. Try dying cloth the natural way, using plants, vegetables, or other natural items.

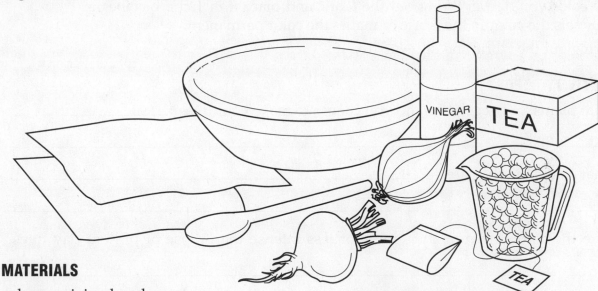

MATERIALS

- large mixing bowls
- knife
- sandwich-size plastic bags
- water
- vinegar
- vegetables and plants of your choice
- long-handled spoon
- small pieces of white or light-colored cotton fabric that have been washed without fabric softener
- strainer
- saucepan
- stove

> ### FASCINATING FACT ★ ★ ★
> Historically, blue and purple were the most highly regarded dye colors. These colors were often worn only by royalty or those with high religious posts. Indigo dyes were in use as long ago as 3,000 B.C.

(continued)

Hands-On History Lab Activity 12 *(continued)*

WHAT TO DO

A. Collect vegetables and plants that you think would make good dye colors. Include onion skins, tea, beets, spinach, cranberries, or goldenrod. Look around the kitchen and outdoors for more choices.

B. Chop up the items you have chosen very finely. Place each ingredient in a separate plastic bag. Roll the bag on a hard surface to crush the plants and release the color.

C. Place 1 cup of water in a saucepan and add the contents of one of your plastic bags. Boil on low heat until the water is the color you desire. *(SAFETY NOTE: Handle hot materials carefully to avoid burns.)*

D. Remove the liquid from the heat and allow to cool. After stirring the mixture, discard the leftover plant material.

E. Place a small piece of pre-washed cotton into the dye mixture. Stir the cloth until it is totally wet. Allow the cloth to remain in the mixture until it reaches the color you desire. Wring out the fabric and place it in 1 cup of vinegar. This sets the color in the fabric or makes the color permanent.

F. Wring out the fabric and allow to dry.

LAB ACTIVITY REPORT

1. What plants and vegetables did you choose to make your dyes? _____

_____

2. What colors did they create? _____

_____

3. Were the colors of your dyes more or less intense than those of present-day dyes?

_____

DRAWING CONCLUSIONS

4. What colors of dye do you think might have been used most in the area you live?

Explain. _____

_____

5. Why do you think it is important to use pre-washed cotton for your experiments

with dyes? _____

_____

_____

Hands-On History Lab Activity 13

Bandboxes—Moving West

Between 1840 and 1865, 500,000 Americans moved west. Ways of traveling and even luggage have changed drastically since then. Learn more about preparing for travel during this time.

BACKGROUND

Settlers' lives depended on the preparations they made before starting their trip west. The four-month journey required travelers to take most of what they needed with them. There were few places to buy supplies. Valuable possessions were often left behind. Even so, when the going was tough, settlers often had to leave supplies along the trail to lighten the wagons for tired oxen or horses. One popular piece of luggage was the bandbox, a small box made of poster board or thin wooden slats for holding small items. You can make a bandbox like the ones used in the 1800s.

MATERIALS

- pencil
- paper
- scissors
- paper clips
- ruler
- 8" × 9" poster board
- 6½" × 5¼" poster board
- glue
- wrapping paper
- glue stick

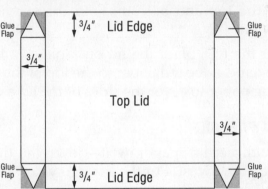

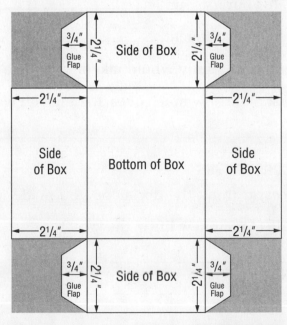

(continued)

Hands-On History Lab Activity 13 (continued)

WHAT TO DO

A. Enlarge and cut out the pattern on the previous page from the 8″× 9″ piece of poster board. Crease along all the lines, bending all the flaps toward the center. Repeat for the box's top, using the 6½″ × 5¼″ piece of poster board.

B. Glue the flaps to the inside of the box and its lid and secure with paper clips while the glue dries. Allow the glue to dry completely.

C. Lay a 3¼″ × 16¾″ strip of wrapping paper on a table, decorative side down, with the long side facing you. Mark a line ½″ down from the top and bottom. Spread glue over one of the box's sides. Position the glue-covered box side, on the wrapping paper strip between the two lines you have drawn and about ½″ from the left edge of the wrapping paper. Then spread glue on each remaining side and rotate the box until all the sides are wrapped. Clip the paper downward at each corner of the box where the paper extends beyond the top and bottom. Fold the extensions over the edge and glue them down.

D. To cover the top, place the lid on a piece of wrapping paper, trace, and cut out the shape. Glue the paper to the top of the lid. Use a 1¾″ × 17½″ piece of wrapping paper to cover the sides of the lid as you did with the box sides.

LAB ACTIVITY REPORT

1. On a small piece of paper, write down the things you might pack in your bandbox if you were going west. Put the list into your box. Exchange your box with a partner.

How were your lists similar? _____

How were they different? _____

2. List items your family would take if you were traveling west in a covered wagon (Be

sure to estimate how much of each thing you would need.) _____

_____

DRAWING CONCLUSIONS

3. How do you think the decisions you made about what supplies to take with you

would affect your new life in the West? _____

_____

_____

Name _____ Date _____ Class _____

Quill and Ink

From the 1500s until the 1800s, most people wrote documents using quill pens, made from the large feathers of geese or swans. Try to make a quill pen and natural inks, and you can write and draw as our ancestors did.

BACKGROUND

Beautiful handwriting was important in the 1800s. Letters were more than just a means of communication. They were an expression of special regard for the people who received them. The more detailed the handwriting the better. Children and adults often wrote in diaries called *monitors*. They recorded the weather or daily activities, but rarely revealed their thoughts and feelings. Ink was not always available so writers made it from such things as walnut shells or berries. Because these inks faded over time, original documents are often hard to find and read. Pens, too, were homemade.

CRANBERRY INK RECIPE

- 1 cup fresh cranberries
- 2 tablespoons water
- medium saucepan
- metal spoon
- cheesecloth
- clean container with lid

WALNUT SHELL INK RECIPE

- 4 empty walnut shells
- 1 cup water
- ½ teaspoon salt
- 1 teaspoon vinegar
- paper bag
- hammer
- saucepan
- cheesecloth
- clean container with lid

MATERIALS

- ink recipes
- stove
- writing paper

Quill Pen

- 8–10" feather (available at most craft stores)
- small craft knife or scissors
- warm, soapy water
- small piece of felt

FASCINATING FACT ★ ★ ★

The first ballpoint pen was made by John H. Loud in 1888. Today, about 2 billion ballpoint pens are manufactured in the United States each year.

(continued)

WHAT TO DO

A. To make cranberry ink Place the cranberries and water in a saucepan. Bring the mixture to a boil. *(SAFETY NOTE: Handle hot materials carefully to avoid burns.)* Crush the cranberries with the spoon to release their color. Allow the mixture to cool. Place a piece of cheesecloth over the container. Carefully pour the mixture into the container. The cheesecloth will strain out the crushed cranberries. Seal with a lid.

B. To make walnut shell ink Place the shells in a paper bag and crush with the hammer. Put the crushed shells in the saucepan and add the water. Bring the mixture to a boil. Add the salt and vinegar to set the ink. Turn down the heat and allow the mixture to simmer for 30 minutes. Cool. Strain the ink through the cheesecloth into the container. Keep the mixture tightly covered and avoid getting it on your clothes or hands. It stains.

C. To make a quill pen Soak the feather in warm soapy water for 15 minutes. Trim about 2" of feathers off along the shaft at the bottom end of the feather. Cut off the end of the feather's shaft at an angle to form the nib, or point, of the pen. *(SAFETY NOTE: Cut on heavy cardboard and handle sharp tools with care to avoid cuts.)* Use a straight pin to clean out the inside of the quill. Be careful not to crack the nib. Cut a small slit in the center of the nib to help control the ink flow. Dip the nib into ink, blot on a small piece of felt, and you are ready to write.

D. Practice with your quill pen and homemade inks on a sheet of writing paper.

LAB ACTIVITY REPORT

1. What color ink did the walnut shells make? _____

2. Which kind of ink worked the best in your tests? _____

DRAWING CONCLUSIONS

3. Do you think it would take you much longer to do your homework if you had to use

   quill pens and homemade inks? Why? _____

   _____

   _____

4. Was your handwriting neater or messier with the quill pen and homemade inks?

   _____

   _____

Hands-On History Lab Activity 15

Saltwater Taffy Pull

Making candy was often a social event in the early 1800s. Young people would gather and as a group make candy to be enjoyed for the evening. Try to recreate a taffy pull.

BACKGROUND

Taffy pulls were a popular gathering for young people. Guests would pull the golden, warm taffy into ropes and then cut the candy and eat it. Candy making, especially taffy pulls, became a family or social event because it required constant attention and many hands to stir and pull the taffy. Candy was a luxury that was rarely available in the stores. You can recreate this old time social event.

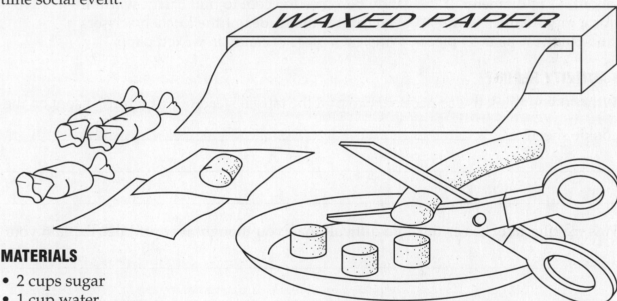

MATERIALS

- 2 cups sugar
- 1 cup water
- 2 tablespoons butter or margarine, softened
- 2 teaspoons vanilla
- 1 cup light corn syrup
- 1½ teaspoons salt
- food coloring (optional)
- extra butter
- 2 quart saucepan
- kitchen scissors
- large flat pan or cookie sheet
- waxed paper
- candy thermometer
- stove

> ### FASCINATING FACT ★ ★ ★
>
> The average American eats 18 pounds of candy annually. More than 2,000 different kinds of candy are manufactured in the United States, and more than half of these candies are made with chocolate!

(continued)

Hands-On History Lab Activity 15 (continued)

WHAT TO DO

A. Butter the cookie sheet. In the saucepan combine the sugar, corn syrup, water, and salt. Heat the mixture to boiling over medium heat. Carefully stir until the sugar is dissolved. Place the candy thermometer in the pan and heat the mixture until the temperature reaches 262°F. *(SAFETY NOTE: Handle hot materials carefully to avoid burns.)*

B. Remove from the heat. Stir in the butter, vanilla, and food coloring (if desired). Pour onto the cookie sheet. Let cool 10 to 15 minutes until the taffy is cool enough to handle. Wash your hands very well and coat your hands with butter.

C. Divide the mixture in half with your hands. With a partner pull and twist each half until the candy holds its shape. Pull the taffy into long ropes about ¾″ in diameter. If the candy becomes too cool to pull easily, warm it for a few minutes in a 350° oven. Butter the blades of the kitchen scissors and cut the rope in 1″ pieces. Wrap each piece of candy in waxed paper.

LAB ACTIVITY REPORT

1. Why do you think it was necessary to pull the taffy instead of just letting it cool on the cookie sheet? _____

_____

_____

2. Was making taffy easier or more difficult than you thought it would be? Explain your answer. _____

_____

DRAWING CONCLUSIONS

3. How long did it take to make the taffy? How often do you think making candy would occur today if it took this long to make? _____

_____

_____

4. How did your taffy taste? Did you like it as well as commercially produced candies?

_____

_____

Hands-On History Lab Activity 16

Making Carbonated Drinks

During the mid-1800s sweetened soda water became increasingly familiar. Sweet water was originally made in large vats, or containers, in people's kitchens. Try to make ginger-flavored soda in your kitchen.

BACKGROUND

Carbonated water was once thought to heal illnesses. People went to springs for the sparkling water. Adding herbs and sweeteners made the water taste better, and soda pop was born. All soda pops have three basic ingredients: carbonated water, sweetener, and flavoring. People made soda pop at home from ingredients they could find locally. Old-time soda pop tasted much stronger than today's soft drinks, and flavors varied from home to home and batch to batch. Because soda pop was still believed to be a healthful tonic, pharmacies in larger cities sold soda pop by the glass. Some of the brews made in the 1800s are still available today. Mr. Hire's root beer recipe was perfected in 1876 and has not changed since. People used soda pop extracts to make their own sodas, and the last packets of extracts were sold in 1983. To make soda pop at home today, you have to do it the old-fashioned way!

MATERIALS

- 4 quarts water
- large pot with lid
- 3 tablespoons ginger, fresh or powdered
- juice from ½ lime
- 2½ cups sugar
- 3 tablespoons cream of tartar
- 1 tablespoon baker's yeast
- coffee filter
- long-handled spoon
- funnel
- stove
- clean, empty gallon milk container
- hammer
- refrigerator

> ### FASCINATING FACT ★ ★ ★
> Coca-Cola™ is the number one selling soft drink in the world. People ask for Coke 335 million times a day in more than 155 countries.

(continued)

Hands-On History Lab Activity 16 *(continued)*

WHAT TO DO

A. Put 4 quarts of boiling water into a large pot and bring it to a boil. Add the ginger, lime juice, and sugar to the boiling water. *(SAFETY NOTE: Handle hot materials carefully to avoid burns.)* If you use fresh ginger, cut the ginger into slices and use the hammer to bruise them gently to release the flavor. Stir the mixture very well. When the sugar is dissolved, add the cream of tartar and stir well again. Allow the mixture to cool until it is lukewarm. (A drop or two dripped on the inside of your wrist will feel just slightly warm.) Then add the baker's yeast. Note: If the mixture is too hot, it will kill the yeast and carbonation will not form. Cover the pot and let the soda sit for 6 hours.

B. Pour the mixture into the plastic milk container through a funnel lined with a coffee filter to strain out particles. Do not fill the jug all the way to the top. You need to leave 2" to 3" of space so that carbon dioxide can collect. Filling the jug too full may cause the lid to pop off when the pressure builds up. Place the soda in the refrigerator, tightly capped. For the best taste, wait two days before sampling your soda pop.

LAB ACTIVITY REPORT

1. What does the ginger soda taste like? Is it different from the soda you buy? _____

_____

_____

2. Why is it necessary to leave room at the top of the jug? _____

_____

_____

DRAWING CONCLUSIONS

3. Baker's yeast is also used in making bread. From your observations, what do you think

the yeast does to the bread dough? _____

_____

4. If you leave the top off your soda, will it lose its carbonation? What conclusion can you

reach from this observation? _____

_____

_____

Testing A Fort Sumter Model

As Southern states began seceding from the Union, Americans' thoughts turned to war. The shots fired at Fort Sumter began America's most deadly conflict. To a great degree, victory depended on the resources each side brought to the war effort.

BACKGROUND

With the election of Abraham Lincoln in 1860, Southern states seceded from the United States to form the Confederate States of America. With the nation divided in two parts, forts along the borders prepared for war. Early forts were often nothing more than four log walls with tall blockhouses at each corner. Soldiers used the blockhouses as lookouts and for shooting. The Civil War's most famous fort, Fort Sumter, stood at the entrance to the harbor of Charleston, South Carolina. You can make a model of Fort Sumter to help you understand how these forts functioned.

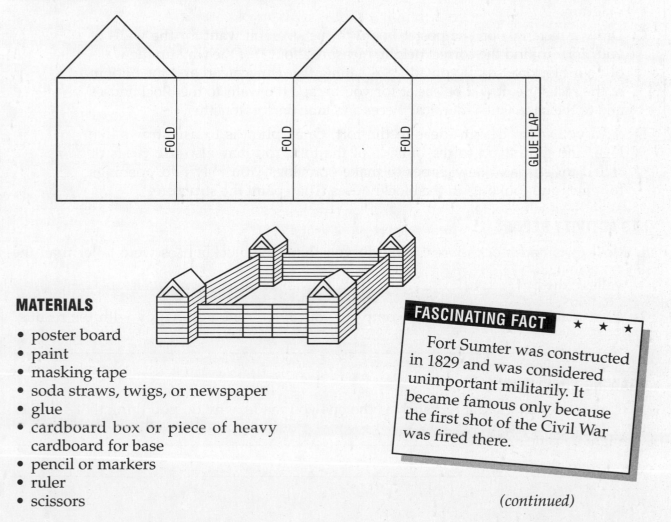

FOLD   FOLD   FOLD   GLUE FLAP

MATERIALS

- poster board
- paint
- masking tape
- soda straws, twigs, or newspaper
- glue
- cardboard box or piece of heavy cardboard for base
- pencil or markers
- ruler
- scissors

FASCINATING FACT ★ ★ ★

Fort Sumter was constructed in 1829 and was considered unimportant militarily. It became famous only because the first shot of the Civil War was fired there.

(continued)

WHAT TO DO

A. Begin by sketching an outline of the fort's outer walls on the cardboard you will use for a base. Remember that the blockhouses should stand much taller than the walls of the rest of the fort. Make sure that the basic walls of the fort and those of the blockhouses are squares. Use the pattern shown in the diagram and draw the pattern for the blockhouses onto the poster board. Cut 4 identical pieces from the poster board, using this pattern. Then fold as shown on the diagram to make the walls of the blockhouses. Tuck the flap inside the walls and tape with masking tape.

B. Next make the roofs for your blockhouses. Fold a piece of poster board in half and use one of the squares on the diagram as a pattern for the roof. Lay the pattern on the poster board with one edge against the fold. Enlarge the pattern by about ¼" on each of the 3 sides that are not against the fold. Cut the roof piece; then use that piece as a pattern for 3 more pieces. Place pieces over the blockhouses with the fold matching the peaks and tape the roofs to the blockhouses. Set your blockhouses in position on your diagram.

C. Draw a rectangle on the poster board to the size you want for the walls of your fort. To find the correct height, measure about ⅔ of the way up the walls of your blockhouses. If you add a ½" taping flap to each end and the bottom of the rectangle, it will be easier for you to tape the walls to the blockhouses and to the base. Cut 4 identical pieces and tape the fort together.

D. Add your own design ideas to the fort. One option is to use straws like logs, and glue them to the outside of the fort. You may also use twigs or rolled up strips of newspaper to make your logs. You may add openings for gates and lookouts in the blockhouses. Then paint the structure.

LAB ACTIVITY REPORT

1. Most forts had blockhouses. Why do you think the blockhouses were taller than the

walls of the fort? _____

2. What materials did you use to complete your fort? Were you happy with the results?

_____

DRAWING CONCLUSIONS

3. If an enemy attacked a fort such as the one you made, why do you think that supplies

might become an issue? _____

_____

Hands-On IIistory Lab Activity 18

Civil War Resource Puzzle

Although there were many reasons that the Civil War ended with a Union victory, the North's resources were one of the most important. Make a resource puzzle map of the United States during the Civil War to help you understand the role resources played in the war.

BACKGROUND

The Civil War erupted in 1861 and caused more American casualties than any other war in history. As state after state seceded, borders were vitally important to both sides of the conflict. Each state held important resources that could influence the outcome of the war. The North had more material resources, but the Southern states truly believed in the Confederate cause and had a great military tradition. Create a puzzle that highlights the resources each side brought to the war.

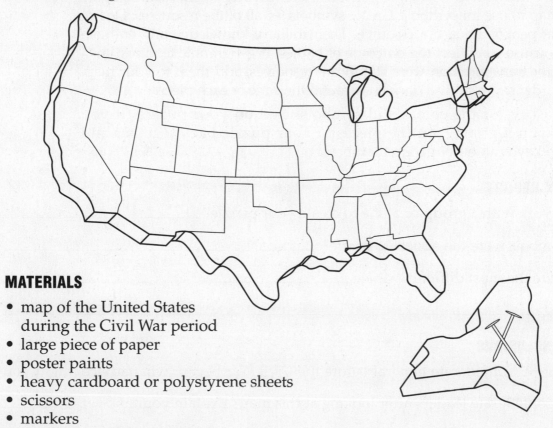

MATERIALS
- map of the United States during the Civil War period
- large piece of paper
- poster paints
- heavy cardboard or polystyrene sheets
- scissors
- markers
- textbook, research materials
- variety of objects to represent resources (optional)

(continued)

Hands-On History Lab Activity 18 *(continued)*

WHAT TO DO

A. Copy an outline of the United States on a large piece of paper. Make your map large enough so that each state has room for resource symbols. Outline the states and territories on your map. This is the base for the puzzle.

B. Trace the shape of each state and territory on the cardboard and carefully cut them out. Place each of the shapes on the cardboard to make sure they fit together. Reshape them as needed.

C. Paint the Confederate states, Union states, and territories different colors. Label each piece of your puzzle with the name of the state or territory. If you want to make this a group project, you may give each group member one of the puzzle pieces for which to do research and create symbols. Use your textbook and other research materials to identify major resources that different states brought to the war. For example, New York had a manufacturing base. On the New York piece of the puzzle, you might draw a gear to symbolize manufacturing. Or you might find small objects, such as small screws, that you can glue to your map to use for symbols. Create symbols for all of the resources. Do not forget that people are also a resource. Their military knowledge and enthusiasm for a cause can affect the outcome of battles. If geographic features, such as rivers for transportation were significant resources, add them to your map. On the border states draw a dark line around the edge of each piece.

D. Include a key for the colors and symbols used on your puzzle. If you worked with a group, put the pieces of your puzzle back together and create the key with other group members.

LAB ACTIVITY REPORT

1. Did you work with a group or alone to create your puzzle? _____

2. Which symbols were the easiest to create? _____

3. Which were the most difficult? _____

_____

DRAWING CONCLUSIONS

4. If you were a Confederate general before the Civil War began, what advice might you give the Confederate leaders after looking at this map? Explain your answer. _____

_____

5. What generalizations can you make about where the resources of the United States were concentrated during this period? _____

_____

Hands-On History Lab Activity 19

Hoop Races

Did you ever wonder what young people did with their time before radio, television, movies, and video games were invented? During the late 1800s, hoop rolling was a popular activity. You can re-create this old-fashioned toy and try your skill at an activity that might test your understanding of physics.

BACKGROUND

Children have always found ways to test their skills in activities that are appropriate to their time and location. Yesterday's balls, hoops, and sticks were like today's rollerblades, skateboards, and video games. Children in the late 1800s became amazingly skillful at using a stick to roll a large hoop down a twisting path without allowing the hoop to fall over.

The original hoop was usually made from hoops used on a discarded keg or barrel. The stick was just a piece of wooden lath with a ball or block attached. Hoop rolling took skill and practice, and the game had many variations. Try to make a hoop and stick and play some of the games of the nineteenth century.

MATERIALS

- Cable tubing or plastic conduit, 78 inches long and ¾" in diameter
- 20" long wooden dowel, or rod, ⅜" in diameter
- 2" wooden dowel, or rod, ⅜" in diameter
- ¾" wooden ball (the first four items are available in hardware stores)
- white glue
- 1¼" nail
- paint (optional)
- paintbrush (optional)
- wire cutter
- hammer

FASCINATING FACT ★ ★ ★

Toys were almost entirely handcrafted until the late eighteenth century. Mass-produced toys became available for the first time then. Mechanical, metal toys appeared during the 1800s. Before this time items such as music boxes were owned only by adults because they were so expensive.

(continued)

Hands-On History Lab Activity 19 *(continued)*

WHAT TO DO

A. Apply glue on half of the 2″ dowel. Push the glued end into one end of the tubing. Apply glue to the rest of the dowel. Loop the rest of the tubing around to form a hoop and push the dowel into the other end of the tubing. The two ends should meet snugly. Wipe off any excess glue and allow the glue to dry. This is your hoop.

B. If desired, paint the wooden ball and 20″ dowel and allow to dry. Then hammer the nail into the center of the wooden ball. Cut off the head of the nail using the wire cutters. Pound the headless nail into the 20″ dowel by hammering on the wooden ball. (See illustration.) Center the ball on the dowel and pound until the ball and dowel are snugly together. The stick is used to correct the direction of the hoop as you roll it.

C. **Hoop Races:** Set up a course with a starting and finishing line. Try putting some twists and turns into the course. Put markers a couple of feet apart along the edges of the course. See how fast you can roll the hoop through the course without tipping the hoop over or losing control of it. Now try rolling the hoop using other ways to control it, such as your hands, or a long piece of string or light rope, threaded through the hoop with one end of the rope held in each hand. Keep a record of which method worked the best.

LAB ACTIVITY REPORT

1. Which parts of constructing the hoop and stick were the most difficult? Explain. _____

_____

2. Which method of rolling the hoop was the easiest? _____

3. Which method was the hardest? _____

4. What was your best time through the course? _____

_____

DRAWING CONCLUSIONS

5. Why do you think this toy was designed using the stick and ball rather than some of

the other methods you tried? _____

_____

6. Was the hoop easier to keep upright when it rolled faster or when it rolled more

slowly? _____

Hands-On History Lab Activity 20

Peanut Butter Mania

Every second someone in the United States or Canada buys a jar of peanut butter. Try making one of America's favorite spreads the old-fashioned way.

BACKGROUND

When the boll weevil, an insect that attacks cotton plants, damaged cotton crops after the Civil War, Southern farmers began to look for a substitute crop. They planted peanuts on more and more acres and researchers looked for new uses for peanuts. In 1890 a doctor who was looking for an easily digestible form of protein for his patients made peanut butter, and the rest, as they say, is history. The peanut butter sandwich became a permanent part of the American diet. Of the 4 billion pounds of peanuts the United States produces each year, half become peanut butter. Even if you don't live in one of the major peanut-producing states of Georgia, Alabama, North Carolina, Texas, Oklahoma, Virginia, and Florida, you can make your own peanut butter. Try making two different batches and compare the results.

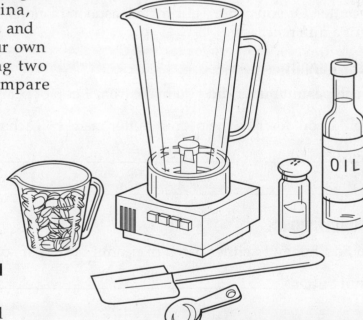

MATERIALS FOR EACH BATCH

- 1 cup shelled peanuts
- 1½ tablespoons peanut oil
- ½ teaspoon salt
- blender or food processor
- heavy rolling pin
- spatula
- plastic container with lid
- crackers or celery
- cinnamon (optional)
- honey (optional)

FASCINATING FACT ★ ★

By the time you graduate from high school, you will probably have eaten about 1,500 peanut butter sandwiches.

(continued)

WHAT TO DO

A. Batch One: Place the peanuts in a blender. Blend for about one minute, or until peanuts are finely chopped. Add the oil and salt and blend until smooth. **Batch Two:** Put a cup of peanuts into a heavy, 1-quart plastic bag with a zipper type closing. Close the bag securely. Then place that bag inside a similar bag, so your peanuts are double bagged. Use the rolling pin to crush the peanuts inside the plastic bag, rolling until they are crushed. Then open the bags and add the oil and salt. Try to remove as much air as possible from the bag. Continue rolling until the peanut butter is of spreading consistency.

B. Try your peanut butter on a cracker or celery stick. Place the remaining peanut butter into covered containers. These peanut butters need to be refrigerated. The oil will separate from the crushed peanuts. Stir well before using to get the best consistency and taste.

C. You can add ¼ cup of honey after grinding the nuts. Just blend into the peanut butter. Or you can try adding a teaspoon of cinnamon to the peanut butter for a different taste.

LAB ACTIVITY REPORT

1. How much peanut butter did you make from 1 cup of peanuts? _____

2. How would you describe the peanut butter made by each method? _____

_____

_____

DRAWING CONCLUSIONS

3. Did you add honey to either batch of peanut butter? If so did it change the texture of

   the peanut butter? _____

_____

4. How would you describe the differences between your peanut butters and the peanut

   butter you buy? _____

_____

5. How do you think making peanut butter commercially affected peanut butter's

   popularity? _____

_____

Hands-On History Lab Activity 21

Creating A World War II Artifact

Great technological advances occurred in the twentieth century. From the first affordable car to computers, technology has drastically changed the way Americans live. Those who lived during World War II have seen rapid changes, but they remember times when technology was just beginning to assume an important role in the military and in the world in general. You can understand what life was like during this time by interviewing and researching an oral history from World War II.

BACKGROUND

On December 7, 1941, the Japanese attacked Pearl Harbor in the Hawaiian Islands forcing the United States into World War II. More than 16 million Americans fought in this war. Many veterans of World War II experienced the desperation of the Great Depression, the challenges of war, and the prosperity of the postwar period. Those at home coped with shortages, rationing, restricted travel, and the loss of loved ones. Their memories of these events represent a personal history of their times. You can help record an oral history of this period.

MATERIALS

- camcorder or other videotaping equipment (optional)
- cassette recorder (optional)
- blank tape or video cassette (optional)
- 3″ × 5″ index cards
- construction paper
- glue or tape
- reference magazines or books on the twentieth century

FASCINATING FACT ★ ★
In the years following World War II, 77,000,000 babies were born. Members of this group have been nick-named "Baby Boomers."

(continued)

WHAT TO DO

A. Use your textbook and other resources to identify questions you would like to ask about this period. On 3″ × 5″ index cards, write the questions you would like to ask your interviewee. Some interesting topics might include technological changes that occurred during his or her lifetime, memories of the war years and how they affected lives, or other changes that occurred once the war was over. Organize your questions logically.

B. Pick at least two older family members, friends, or neighbors to interview about the war years, or call a local nursing home to see if one of the residents might give you an interview. Be sure to ask the same questions of each person you interview.

C. Use a camcorder or cassette recorder to tape the interview if you choose.

D. Find pictures from magazines and books to illustrate the events that your interviewees spoke of. Create a scrapbook using construction paper and copies of the pictures. Share your scrapbook with the class as you present interesting portions of your interview.

LAB ACTIVITY REPORT

1. What did your subjects tell you that you did not know or that surprised you? _____

_____

2. Were the answers to your questions the same from both interviews? _____

_____

3. Did it make a difference whether your interviewees were male or female? Explain.

_____

4. If you were going to do additional interviews, what other questions might you ask?

_____

DRAWING CONCLUSIONS

5. Your recorded interviews might be considered primary sources about these times because they are told by people who actually witnessed certain of these events. From your experience what conclusions can you draw about using primary sources to study history?

_____

_____

ACTIVITY 1

1. Hawaiian Islands, Pacific Coast, Intermountain Region, Rocky Mountains, Interior Plains, Canadian Shield, Appalachian Mountains, Coastal Plains

2. Answers will vary. Look for evidence that students have considered the physical characteristics of the United States as well as the proximity of the United States to other countries.

3. Answers will vary. Look for evidence of critical thinking about the technologies that are available and their uses. Students should be aware that even with the availability of transportation, exploration is very difficult and time-consuming.

4. Answers will vary, but should include appropriate geographic references to landforms, soil types, and water resources.

5. Answers will vary, but should accurately reflect community makeup.

ACTIVITY 2

1. Answers will vary depending on geographic location, but answers could include berries, peaches, apples, plums, grapes, and other local fruits.

2. Accept all reasonable answers, such as pumpkins, squashes, meats, maize, beans, sunflowers, and nuts.

3. The water is evaporated out of the fruit; sugars are therefore more concentrated.

4. The high concentrations of sugars and the lack of moisture retards the growth of spoilage organisms. Since water is heavy, dried fruit weighs less so it is easier to transport than fresh fruit.

5. Fruits, including raisins, and meats such as jerky are still preserved by drying. These foods are probably still dried because the drying process concentrates flavors. They also are easier to transport.

ACTIVITY 3

1. Answers will vary, but could include electricity, running water, phone service, and grocery stores.

2. Pioneers rose with the sun to make full use of the sunlight that was available to complete their chores. Retiring early helped conserve precious candles.

3. Answers will vary, but could include reading, homework, playing sports. Look for evidence of thought beyond the obvious answers. Changes in lifestyle could include an earlier bedtime or more time spent with family.

4. Mirrors and polished metal reflected more of the candles' light into the room. Since candlelight is very dim and candles are expensive, pioneers needed to make the best use of what light they had.

ACTIVITY 4

1. 25–30 minutes

2. Answers will vary. Since homemade ice cream lacks stabilizers, it melts more readily into a liquid. This characteristic changes the way the ice cream feels in the mouth. Flavors may taste fresher.

3. Answers will vary, but could include flavoring agents such as chocolate, fruits, and nuts. Abler students may note that commercial ice cream is often foamier; contains stabilizers; and often has a lower fat content than the early American variety.

4. Salt water freezes solid at a lower temperature than freshwater. Adding salt to the solution keeps the solution cold, but in a liquid form, so the can will turn readily in the solution.

ACTIVITY 5

1. Answers will vary, but look for evidence of research being done on who were typical American settlers.

2. Answers will vary, but could include lack of food, unfamiliar diseases, hard work, leaving family behind, and the lack of luxuries.

3. Answers will vary, but look for evidence of critical thinking on a variety of aspects of the students' everyday life.

ACTIVITY 6

1. Research should reveal that periods of indenture were usually 3–7 years.
2. Answers will vary, but look for evidence of research; students might be surprised, for example, to learn that indentured young women often received household goods, such as feather beds or cooking utensils at the end of their terms; young men received tools related to their work so they could earn their own livings.
3. Answers will vary. Look for evidence of critical thinking and use of parallels and differences between today's children's lives and those of an indentured child.
4. Answers will vary. Students might note that past jobs were more often manual trades that lent themselves to training by doing. Still, school-to-work programs continue to have elements of mentoring like former apprenticeship programs did.

ACTIVITY 7

1. 10 to 20 minutes for butter to form; another 10 minutes for shaping
2. Answers will vary, but should maintain a rhythm to churn butter by.
3. Answers will vary, but could include a variety of chores such as gathering eggs and berries, babysitting, weeding gardens, fetching water, and other farm and household chores.
4. Answers will vary, but might include bread, cookies, ice cream, soups, and a variety of other foods.
5. Answers will vary, but may include better transportation, larger cities, busier schedules, fewer home helpers, more working women.

ACTIVITY 8

1. Answers will vary. Look for reasonable judgments.
2. Answers will vary. Likely choices are rabbit, deer, or raccoon.
3. Native Americans used paints and pigments made from natural resources such as plants, berries, and minerals. Students will use poster paints and mix their own colors or markers.
4. Answers will vary, but should reflect the students' artwork.

5. Answers will vary, but should show evidence of critical thinking about the differences of perspectives between the colonists and the Native American culture.

ACTIVITY 9

1. Soap was made of fat, ashes, and water.
2. Pioneer soap was harsher; soap made from scraps still contains modern ingredients such as moisturizers and perfumes. The actual process of turning fats into soaps has already been done by the time the soap scraps are turned into a fresh bar of soap so the smell of lye and animal fats is missing.
3. Answers will vary. Students may have very different experiences with their soap depending on the kinds of soap scraps they used.
4. Answers will vary. Students might mention that modern soap-making methods have made soap more readily available and changed our attitudes about cleanliness. Abler students will be aware of the implications in other areas such as health care, and in specialized soaps for industrial applications.

ACTIVITY 10

1. Answers will vary, but should reflect an understanding of the issues involved.
2. Answers will vary, but should include comments that show how reducing issues to campaign slogans is a difficult process. Abler students will recognize that slogans may be effective tools for calling attention to the candidates and parties, but they treat issues only superficially.
3. Answers will vary, but should include a discussion of the advantages and limitations of election slogans as opposed to those of televised materials, such as increased accountability, limited time, number of exposures, etc.
4. Answers will vary, but students will probably mention radio and television spots or newspaper ads.

ACTIVITY 11

1. to teach the alphabet and how to stitch
2. Answers will vary, depending on how complex the design is.
3. Answers will vary, but should include that children learned on samplers and children today learn with pencil, paper, and computers.

These items were not available in early American history.

4. Answers will vary, but might include educational TV, computer games, reading, movies, and CD-ROMS.

ACTIVITY 12

1. Answers will vary, but should include several plant ingredients.
2. Answers will vary depending on what dyeing agent was used.
3. Present-day dyes are usually more intense.
4. Answers should show evidence of critical thinking and include products that are naturally found in the students' environment.
5. Pre-washing removes anything that might make the color uneven such as sizing or softeners. Cotton accepts dyes better than synthetic fibers. Also, pioneers used natural yarns.

ACTIVITY 13

1. Answers will vary. Bandboxes often held shirt collars, but jewelry, trinkets, ribbons, lace, and other small items are also acceptable.
2. Answers will vary. Look for evidence that students have considered both the trip and the establishment of a new home. Food stuffs, cooking utensils, sewing supplies, mirrors and trinkets for trade, medicines, clothing, tools, and seeds are some possibilities.
3. Answers will vary. Look for evidence of critical thinking about the task of starting fresh in a new environment. Students should be aware that supplies were very scarce and if certain things were not taken along, settlers had to do without. Things such as seeds, tools, and sewing supplies might help settlers to live off the land.

ACTIVITY 14

1. Walnut shells make brown ink.
2. Walnut shell ink
3. Answers will vary but should recognize how improvements in writing instruments have changed the way information is recorded.
4. Answers will vary, but students will probably find writing is messier with a quill pen.

ACTIVITY 15

1. Pulling taffy introduces air into the mixture and makes the taffy more pliable.
2. Answers will vary, but students will probably find that it was more difficult than they thought.
3. Answers will vary, but should be at least a half an hour. Most will answer that candy would not be made very often.
4. Answers will vary. Homemade candies usually are fresher which improves taste. If the candy is not what students are used to, however, they may prefer the familiar to the fresh.

ACTIVITY 16

1. Answers will vary according to how much flavoring agent students used.
2. Room must be allowed at the top of the jug for carbon dioxide to gather.
3. Answers will vary. Students should realize that the carbon dioxide bubbles that form in the soda also form in bread dough. The bubbles are then trapped in the dough, making it rise and giving bread its texture.
4. When the cap is left off the soda, there is no pressure inside the bottle to keep the bubbles (carbon dioxide gas) suspended in the liquid. Since the gas is lighter than the liquid, it simply rises and escapes into the air.

ACTIVITY 17

1. Blockhouses were used as places to shoot from and as lookouts. Therefore the additional height gave soldiers an advantage over an enemy approaching on foot or horseback.
2. Answers will vary depending on which materials students chose. Twigs might give the most realistic appearance, but finding straight twigs and cutting them to size would be more difficult than using the other materials. The process, however, would be more authentic. Drinking straws might be the easiest, but plastic straws are more difficult to paint. Rolled strips of newspaper are more time consuming. Students might also choose other materials.
3. Answers will vary, but students should realize that forts not only kept enemies out, but also kept soldiers inside. A long siege might mean that soldiers ran out of food, water, ammunition, and medical supplies

ACTIVITY 18

1. Answers will vary, but should accurately reflect the process students used.
2. Answers will vary, but should accurately reflect the map.
3. Answers will vary, but should accurately reflect the map.
4. Answers will vary. The Southern states seceded to protect a way of life that was largely agricultural. Northern factories turned out the machinery of the war. The North also had a larger population and, therefore, a larger group from which soldiers could be recruited. After studying the map, students might advise against the war. Some might suggest that the South develop their industries before embarking on a course that could lead to defeat. Some might suggest that the South plan more carefully to obtain the materials they would need, such as stockpiling of war materials and food.
5. Answers will vary, but students may observe that the Civil War resources were concentrated in the Northeast.

ACTIVITY 19

1. Answers will vary. Students who are unfamiliar with tools may find constructing the stick and knob most difficult.
2. Answers will vary. Students might find that it was easier to control the hoop with their hands, but that they would have to stand beside the hoop to roll it without accidentally kicking it or getting it tangled in their feet. Using a rope or string might keep the hoop upright, but would make it very difficult to control and roll with any speed. Using the stick would be faster once they learned the technique.
3. Answers will vary, but students may conclude that the stick method is more difficult to learn, but more efficient.
4. Time will vary depending on the length of the course and the skill that students have in rolling the hoop.
5. Answers will vary. Students may find that it takes practice to keep the hoop upright and rolling, but that the stick and ball allows them to remain the correct distance from the hoop and to run with it without the danger of kicking it or knocking it over. The stick and ball probably allow the best control and speed.

Some may find the activity challenging enough that they will continue to practice.
6. The hoop will stay upright when it rolls faster. At slow speeds it tips more easily.

ACTIVITY 20

1. Answers will vary, but will probably be from one-half to three-fourths cup.
2. Answers will vary. Students might note that the peanut butter made using a blender is smoother, while the hand-rolled variety is more like crunchy style peanut butter. Making peanut butter with a blender is easier and faster. Students might observe that almost anything done the old-fashioned way takes longer. Taste will be a matter of personal preference.
3. Adding honey to the peanut butter not only makes it sweeter, but also has a slight emulsifying action. Peanut butter with honey may be less likely to separate.
4. Answers will vary. Commercial peanut butters may be more uniform and sweeter. Students' peanut butter may taste more like fresh peanuts.
5. They made it more popular.

ACTIVITY 21

1. Answers will vary greatly, but should be consistent with the material in the interview.
2. Answers will vary depending on the questions and the interviewee.
3. Male interviewees might have more firsthand information about the war itself if they had participated. Since most women were not in the armed forces during this period, their comments might reflect what was happening at home.
4. Answers will vary, but might reflect questions that other students asked in connection with the presentation of the scrapbook and tapes.
5. Answers will vary. Some students may find the process of interviewing someone who has actually lived in a historic period makes history more real. Since interviewees may give very different answers to the questions students ask, students might realize that secondary sources, such as textbooks, are based on many such sources, each of whom views history from a particular viewpoint.